Wolf Tracks on the Welcome Mat

Also by Paul Zarzyski

Call Me Lucky
The Make-Up of Ice
Tracks
Roughstock Sonnets
The Garnet Moon
I Am Not a Cowboy
All This Way for the Short Ride
Blue Collar Light
Words Growing Wild—a CD

Wolf Tracks on the Welcome Mat

Poems
Paul Zarzyski

An Imprint of
Carmel Publishing Company

Carmel Publishing Company
PO Box 126, Cedarville, CA 96104
800/731-3322
email bmarch@frontiernet.net
© Carmel Publishing Company

Design: Bunne Hartmann
Hartmann Design Group

Cataloguing in Publication Data
Library of Congress Control Number: 2003111369

Zarzyski, Paul
Wolf Tracks on the Welcome Mat
p. cm. ISBN 1-886312-21-4

First Edition

10 9 8 7 6 5 4 3 2 1

For Friend, Wallace McRae

CONTENTS

1 - FACE-TO-FACE   **1**

Face-To-Face   3
The Meaning of Intimacy   7
Birds in the Stove   8
Little Noises   10
Morning Talk Show   11
Heart's Dressage   12
The Garnet Moon   15
Las Ballenas de Bahia Magdalena   16
Wings   17
Playing Favorites   18
Flight   19

2 - BUCKS IN RUT   **23**

Bucks in Rut   24
Carnivore   29
This Poem, This Predator   30
Montana's Mistral   32
Equine Houdini   34
Putting the Rodeo *Try* into Cowboy Poetry   36
Living in Snake Country   38
The Day the War Began   40
Old Sorrel Mare Turning More and More Roan   41
Feeding the Creatures I Used to Eat   42
Tender   43
Tracks   44

3 - I BELIEVE   **47**

I Believe   49
Shoes   53
Angelina, My Noni's Name, Means *Messenger*   55
Tsankawi   56
On My Birthday, The Serpent—   58
How the Beluga Spoons   59
To Gerald Fuentes—May Heaven Swoon for Him
  Her Handsomest Storybook Bevy   60
Montana Second Hand   62
Imperfect Strangers   64
Manners   66
The Hand   67
Pathetic Fallacy   68
Wolf Tracks on the Welcome Mat   70

4 - ANTIPASTO!   **73**

Antipasto!   75
Bringing Home the Poems   79
Potatoes   81
Running On Empty   84
Pheromones   86
Bizarzyski—Mad Bard and Carpenter Savant
  of Manchester, Montana—Feeds the Finicky Birds   88
The Tumbleweed Munchies   90

Cowboys & Indians   92
Cedarville Sweet   94
Great Harvest Bread, Rock-'n'-Roll-'n'-God   96
Sister Sundays   98
Gardens   100
*I Thought That Hope **Was** Home*   102
Words Growing Wild in the Woods   104

5 - GRACE   **107**

Grace   109
Love the Color of Trout   113
For the Stories   114
Light   116
Firewood   118
The Antler Tree   120
Measuring   122
1998   124
Flashback   126
For One Micro-Chronon of Time   128
Bless the Gentle   130
One Sweet Evening Just This Year   132

1

FACE-TO-FACE

*If what distinguishes us from other members
of the animal kingdom is speech, then literature—
and poetry in particular, being the highest form of
locution—is, to put it bluntly, the goal of our species.*

— Joseph Brodsky

Face-To-Face

Out of nowhere, you find yourself
placed daily before the fortress,
rustic logs throbbing
something from within
you vaguely recognize
as music—so primal,
so otherworldly in its purpose,
you are at once drawn closer,
cautioned back. Succumb
to ugly logic, to mean-spirited
reason, or religion,
and you, believing you shun
merely the unknown, will flee
unwittingly from beauty. Trust the blood,
however, waltzing to four-part harmony
within the heart, and you will be moved
to witness, through the chinking's
thin fissures, the shadows
of the enchanted. Then, and only then,
might you choose to follow
a force you'll lovingly call your soul
through huge swinging doors
thrown open to the glorious
commotion of it all.

The Meaning of Intimacy

Not reasoning, but romantic
prehistoric instinct
coaxes my whiskered cheek to the bristled
muzzle of a colt working long-stemmed timothy-brome
hay evenly inward. My heart beats brisk
time to the rhythm of grinding teeth
crunching tiny pipettes of perfume—sweet
breath and music piped through the pink
nostrils into February air, so still,
so microscopically cold, I see its molecules
misting leafy green. The simplest poetic gift,
if we listen close, sings to the most
primitive sound churning into vision. Graced,
late last night, I sat in the easy
breathing warmth of cottonwood burning
without the slightest wheeze,
not a single creaking from the pine
joints of the ninety-year-old house. In the whisper
and whiff of fresh pencil lead
pressed firmly into notebook pages
curling, I felt the cat
rest her chin against my wool-
stockinged toes—purring and purring
her aboriginal rhythms into the fur-
bearing nerves of my words.

For Verlena Orr and Georgia

Birds in the Stove

Twice I tried to shin the rusty steel
well casing, 25 feet of vertical cannon barrel
some fire-shy handyman hoisted as a chimney
above the tinderbox homestead. I chickened out
halfway up both times, left it swaying in the blue yonder
without a cowl, its black maw
luring like a birdhouse on its back
mostly young starlings. Fluttering
pinwheels in the hollow
pot belly hunkered in our living room,
fireless throughout July, the birds drummed
to a reverberating world of soot. I'd open the door
slowly, slide my trout net over that shaft
of sudden light they'd flush toward,
snare them in the soft-meshed
mushroom cloud of ash.
                              Hell's bells,
how they'd squall shrill
enough in that hollow room
to shear an eardrum—how they'd twist
with their beaks a mean welt
through cotton gloves, as I'd hold them
an extra few seconds just to feel
their powerful hearts
throbbing in harmony with mine. Coming to love
this daily rite of setting them free,
I'd reverently unhinge my grip, offer them
launching without an inch of plummet
into flight, gray dust
puffs in the wakes
of first wingbeats.
                              One day, the tremolo
thrummed softer, calmer. As I slid
the net over the hatch, nothing
shot for freedom's light. Braced,

I waited, slapped the cast
iron sides with a bare hand and held
my ground in this stand-off
until, working up nerve enough to ease
a peek around the asbestosed edge
I came curious-eye-to-stern-eye
with a sparrow hawk, a burnished gemstone
shining from its mine.
                          Maybe this was
the same bird I'd foiled weeks earlier
after watching, through a porch door, it
perched in ambush
above the bored-out burled entrance
into a cottonwood stob—a purple finch,
her beak filled with insects,
ducking in minutes before. To stronger instinct
than her own survival, she poked her head out,
looked both ways but not up, paused,
then shot from the burl into the predator
clutches just as I burst
in the nick of time from the screen door, hawk
turning loose its prey, both birds
fleeing, all three of us squawking
in flight.
              Like a high priest
reaching for the Eucharist
chalice, I cupped the luminous
kestrel, lifted it with both hands
out of the stove, offered it up
to the wind that delivered it from evil. Winged
heartbeats—graceful, plumed
beings of the galactic
rookeries—stars are the souls of birds
drawn sometimes into the black-hole
rictus of the cosmos,
that stark cold downdraft
holding, for all time, the hot bright light of their bones.

Little Noises

Thatched roof of dead grass
over their honeycombed lair sinkholing,
exposing the raw nerves of tree
not meant to see the light of day, voles
make camp at the base
of my transplanted aspen sapling—spoke-worked
furrows to and from the trunk
like shadows of branches. I fret
they will girdle it, kill it, and so
I set mouse traps, sans bait,
in their getaway runs. Sharp snap
of metal to wood seconds after
my leaf rake claws apart their dwelling,
one trap barely catches a foot
that sets off a squealing
so high-pitched, the horses, snorting
and skittish in the corral
a couple hundred feet away, hear it
long before it pierces
what little peace I'd hoped to harbor
during my shift of yardwork. I turn
the critter free, watch it hobble, broken,
toward its hole, know it will not live. Why is it
every time I try to save one life
I silence another
part of myself slowly dying
within—the crippled cell, the shrill cry
disappearing deeper into a single pore,
the screaming, Lord, the screaming.

For Tom Russell

Morning Talk Show

Mister cricket chirps from the kindling
box in the garage right outside
the back door I step through,
seven a.m., to feed the horses,
to breathe in deeply the world's music
I love most. On some mornings,
if I'm sullen or just plain sad, he quits
the instant he hears the rattle
of door latch and creaky wooden step
between indoor carpet and garage
cement floor. He knows where I am
emotionally, knows when I am cheery and thus
cheers right alongside me. He's learned how
his silence makes me take pause
of my poopy mood. He stops me
in my tracks, makes me stand breathless
waiting for him to finally give in
and grace me with his very best
impersonation of Jack Benny see-
sawing on his violin. I tiptoe off
chuckling toward the horses nickering
rambunctious for their breakfast hay,
a flock of honkers overhead, sharp-shinned hawk
squawking somewhere out of sight,
robins scolding fledglings in the aspens
fantastically clicking
castanet leaves—my world filled with words,
every single one telling it like it is.

Heart's Dressage

With snorts and cowpony caprioles
our four horses pitch
to the barn door's first sixteenth note
squawked into a hoarfrost dawn—their Pavlov-dog
salivary response to chow
kicked-in. They gravitate toward air
with terrible mimickings of their Lipizzan
distant cousins umpteen times removed
and then some. Oh, what I would pay in spades
to feel this spry again, first jump
out of the rack. In my one sweet dream,
I still try to ride spirited horses
across Montana arenas, a nor'easter cheering
from bleacher seats.
                                    Wind
today begs to differ with my wish,
quells my yearning,
reincarnates the wildest of all
roughstock twistings
as peaceful sea breezes, a spray
of daisies across the horse latitudes
where legend tells us
sailors sang their chanteys
to the dead they rolled
over gunnels of livestock boats
into the calm.
                          Fond horse memories
this morning do not trigger
my usual brisk strut
back toward the bucking chutes
after a winning ride. I dance
instead to the Lipizzaner
stallions I once watched
from grandstands at the Last Chance Stampede

arena—ghosts of broncs I almost rode
lording their prowess over me
long past my prime. Arthritic hips pounding,
I sat there, downcast, on a hard plank
and clapped on cue with the crowd
applauding around me.
                              What lured my eye
finally away from the eight whitewashed bucking chutes
across the ring—what snapped my trance
from the sun-bleached pink number 6—
was the cadence of scarlet
leg wraps those horses wore,
their hooves moving bold
as truth in a blur of split-second
purchases to the same loose dirt
stirred by so many bloodlines
down through the ages, down
through the layers. I conjured up
a medley of hoofbeats made
for the sake of war, sport, work,
art. To their vital percussion,
I listened from within
the most acoustically ornate palace
hall where music's purest essence
rides the center.
                        The horsemen in red tails
melded with their mounts through *the airs*
above the ground so smoothly
the gold epaulets of their uniforms
barely moved—*levade, courbette,*
croupade, capriole—then grand finale *piaffe*
between the pillars.
                        Hooves in unison
deliver those whole notes

composed in the cannon bones
of long ago—humus and rich silt
uprooted from the horse
latitudes into flaxen-maned waves,
into air, cloud, rain, this hay
I'm feeding and the heart repeating
its movements through histories
of their worlds, your world, all
our glorious worlds
accompanied by the orchestra of horses.

For Randy Rieman and
Joel Nelson, Horsemen

The Garnet Moon

For Elizabeth Dear

After forking alfalfa to the horses,
you sit with your first cup,
first Tesuque sun easing through
windows in LaBajada red
adobe—like liquid tinted pink,
this cornsilk light runneling over the gentle-
curved sills. You feather
the long fingernail file
through beveled arcs and strokes, deliberate
as the violinist guides the bow. Your hands
cast shadows of dancers
to the flagstone floor—shadowed steam
from your coffee, a gossamer
curtain they make love behind
in a spirit breeze. Could this be
the kachina's silhouette—the sacred omen
we've craved in our lone quests
for the dance perfected?
                    I watch your fingers
whisking alfalfa leaf
from your gold hair, Zia sun
steepening into the room. This afternoon,
in blue sage and cholla along the Rio Grande,
we'll muse over a red ant hill,
smooth as workings of a jeweled watch.
You'll spoon, with the nail of your little finger,
a garnet they've mined
and maneuvered to their granular roof
shingled in glitter—a lone moon you'll choose
from this universe. As you lift it
slowly toward the palm I hold above the hill,
spill it and with your nail tip
roll it across the synapse
of all my nerves, a frenzy of ants
comes to a standstill
in this eclipse of lovers locked perfect for the dance.

Las Ballenas de Bahia Magdalena

Off Baja, the boy manning our skiff
calls this mamma gray whale
La Blanca. The white
dapples both her and her calf,
distracted from their synchronized swim
by the shadow six of us cast
standing in the wobbling craft—six tentacles
sprawling across the chop. How odd,
how gangly this umbra must seem
to the infant glimpse of one so rotund.

Or perhaps the outboard's low idle
purl of propeller
lures the two-ton newborn
to buoy-up to our starboard,
spout his sibilant welcome, nuzzle our gunnel.

The mother rises crosswise to our keel,
thirty feet of her on each side. I cross myself
on impulse, recall catechism and that kill
tally of one whaler's manifest—the harpoon's
kinship to Crucifixion. To this apparition,
to this syzygy of peace with fear
in the presence of such pure forgiveness, I kneel,
reach toward the whale, the warm
opalescent light we are told of
by all those who have died and come back.

Wings

I clench his feathered legs together
like a jilted suitor clings
to a limp bouquet. All his love
nocturnal, in a nightmareless life,
he could not foresee, even with ball-
turret vision, the existence of so much
sterile light and steel—this great gray
owl in shock, deflated,
on a veterinarian table, one wing-
bone, jagged as glass pipette,
broken in two.
                        His eyes, dull bulbs
to the brilliance of this room,
beam nothing of his ominous lore,
his fury at our pluck and probe. Humiliation
quells his outrage for mangled plumes
preened quill by quill
to perfection, each barbule
softly muffling the owl's swoop—this ruffled
breadth of feathers that hid his frailness
for so little flesh.
                        The vet threads
metal pins into the shattered
air-as-marrow miracle, little hope
hollow bone will knit at all, let alone
knit with struts enough for flight. The owl,
exposed and marred, wilted
by so much light, leaves his body
to our last-ditch, taxidermic bid
for immortality. We'll never know
what secret love, what spirit locked within
quill and bone, kept this bird
eternally in blossom—crest feathers
petaled like phlox, ten thousand wings
soaring gorgeous for the dark.

Playing Favorites

The great horned owl quartet—hatch
of voluptuous mums, tufts of downy gray—
gawked at us all spring
from a woodwind cottonwood stob, their mom's
ratcheted clacking to our camera shutter
clicking snapshot after snapshot of her chicks—
an Easter lily's pollen-eyed stamens
spathed in their amphitheater of smooth white.

Once, through our picture-tube window,
we caught them goggling with us into the blue
light of late-show violence on the Zenith. Gazing
back through our own puzzled faces
reflected in the pane, we loved
the eight-moon lure of their eyes,
rejoiced in this brief innocence—peace
bloomed so near our lives.

But after their fledging, I caught myself
shooting like a lunatic from the hip
to the shrill panic-squeal of a rabbit, owls
swooping through the yardlight to the gabled
loft they disappeared into—birdshot-
clatter against cedar shakes
long after the barrel's Indian paintbrush
flame-burst, red as meat, left me shivering.

I fired a full-choke warning shot toward God
to stop the nocturnal loss of cottontails
we loved counting each morning from the kitchen,
our favorite window, their ears turning pink-
veined as Christmas poinsettia
with first sun, my favorite time for plant
and animal, when I write, in favor
of prey, this one page outliving the night.

Flight

I felt a little miffed that first morning
the great horned owl did not return
with her fledgling to their nest in my hollow
balm-of-Gilead tree, to their tabernacle
facing east—gentle buss of sunrise
softening even further the tufted chick
when I tiptoed out to say *good-day*
before my first cup of joe,
one scowling old bird, I thought,
of this earth to another. The dawn greeting
had become a ritual that boosted us,
I deemed, beyond the gloom of Tribune news,
into our more civilized, personable world. And so,
upset by their rude rejection of my good will,
I marched up the coulee to search
the abandoned lambing shed for the nocturnal
birds I felt I deserved to call
my friends. How could they desert me
without so much as one wing beat
of warning?
              Their velvety gray pellets
piled below each rafter perch
and a knife-blade feather preened loose
was all I found on the dirt
floor where I stood stunned
in the dankness of an empty nest. The grimace
of a shrew's ivory crossbones and toothed skull,
hatched from the chasm
of an old dry pellet, made me back away,
frame my face in a paneless window,
and brood.
              Peering into the steep
glacial hillside shingled with limestone and shale,
alive with lichen and bright violet verbena,
I climbed, not stepping on one petal,

to the rim where I raised
my single wing feather
and waited.
        For the first time, I witnessed earth
as painful host, not much hope
for some grand galactic raptor
stooping to pick the globe clean. Out of nowhere
I caught myself wishing for such
heroic stroke, softly brushed
my fingertips across the blossoming
tufts of downy verbena at my side,
and understood the mother owl
as mother earth, yearning,
within orbit and soar,
to rid themselves of me for good.

2

BUCKS IN RUT

Only animals can teach us to trade the poverty
of affluence for the affluence of poverty.

— Barney Nelson

To be tough is to be fragile; to be tender
is to be truly fierce.

— Gretel Ehrlich

Bucks in Rut

Too young to hunt, but old
enough to relish killing,
I dwelled on the animal world
during nights of insomnia
at the camp—a dozen unshaven
snorting men wallowing on cots
away from their women and deliberate
with each slug of liquor.
                How quick
their fingers flicked and snapped
nickel-dime, five-of-a-kind stud
in a ring of lingo, *High/low crisscross split—one-eyed jacks,*
shady lady, and man with the battle-axe
wild. How they pinched and thumbed
their brass ammo into bandoleers, worked
and dry-fired their Winchester
bolt-actions and pumps
to a gallery of buxom pin-ups.
                They craved
nights when the trophy swamp buck
haunting them
in thickets of Graveyard Crick
became the dream they each quaked from—
rifle-crack 4 a.m. reveille of bacon
spattering in black skillets. From that snap
of suspenders, cigarette hack, hangover
grumble and stench of wool
socks steaming close to the stove,
I floundered out under Venus,
polestar, and cold beams of birch
into the clean dark.
                There, stunned
by sudden contrast, I envied
the wives—my mother—dreaming

between line-dried linen
on immense beds all to themselves. How calm
I saw them preserved in birdsong
at dawn—no drumroll of grim lull
before first volley. Worlds away,
among the gentle, how simple
the women slept without our constant
hope for snow, without our lust
to track and kill, to tag
our names to smoldering carcasses,
animal or planet, in a quest to hold
all hearts less hot, less holy, than our own.

Carnivore

After reducing the muledeer buck to meat,
to one freezer shelf of venison,
I load the waste—a Snowboy Apple box
full of backfat, bone, bloodshot scrap,
ribcage and antlerless head—into the pickup
and drive up Soup-pot Coulee
where ranchers for decades have
dragged their winterkilled cattle
and led their spent horses. Among skulls
and pelvises, the empty sockets
poking through a *skiff* of snow,
a doe and her two fawns look
like ghosts-of-Christmas
yard ornaments flocked white by the spray
of a hard chinook wind. I jack
a cartridge into the chamber and fire
to frighten them from the road-
hunters making their last-day swing
before dark. I unload the box,
tip it upside down, lift it off
the jelled mold of carcass parts,
and with my ears still ringing, crawl in low gear
back to the house. How can I not think
of a job well-done, the tenderloins grilled rare
tonight with Chianti and wild rice—
how we kill to eat, and eat
to kill again, and how we love,
between the seasons we set aside for killing,
to see the living
go on living? We owe our prey some grace,
some contemplation of their lives
here with us. I think about the deer,
creatures of habit and caution, tiptoeing
through Soup-pot Coulee, coming down with dusk
to feed in alfalfa fields
near the house—what they must sense
upwind of the ripe red pile and the charcoaled
scent of their own flesh.

This Poem, This Predator

Why was it not pure beauty that caught my eye,
the Muse's blessing, incognito, as usual,
mousing the meadow outside the window
above my writing desk—a young skunk, little threat
to mice or man. Yet, I left the couplet
I was so close to hearing right,
traded my pencil for the 12-gauge I could cradle
more intimately in my arms, strolled
within birdshot range, took a bead
and froze, a piss-poor killer this morning
was I—thinking still about the breath-
stop of a poem I was trying
so hard to breathe
linebreak life into. Syntax—each word
circulates with timing and tempo
through the complex pink lung of syntax,
its millions of air-cell alveoli
like microscopic possibilities for the poem
to become the living. If I thought anything
working the Winchester's trigger
through its minuscule movement
that tripped the hammer that struck the pin
stamping the primer with an *O*
crisper than the Smith-Corona's, I thought
how little love has to do with this
cursory touch, though the echo pealed
surprisingly wonderful inside
the hollow propane tank I used
for a rest. At my desk again, my guts
still ringing with what I had done, I felt
queasy and dazed, finishing off the couplet
that will read falsely to me forever:
        ...landscape is anxious to true itself
                to fit the flesh that lives upon it.
The dead skunk lies flat

in the flat pasture. I watch its white
tail hair whiffling with alfalfa
in the breeze, my own breath
stiff and reeking off this page of black
poetry that stopped one big beautiful heart
beating, to give you back this stinking
bit of living truth.

Montana's Mistral

It pulls in unannounced with blue smoke
pouring from under the hood
and a trunkful of stolen luggage—unwelcomed
as a long-forgotten uncle
sporting an orange jump suit,
the name of some county hoosegow
stenciled in big black
letters on the back. To a nor'easter
pounding down on the log house
all night, I toss, sway, roll, throw
my arms, restless as ponderosa
on an open slope. *Buffalo,*
I tell myself, *not sheep*—dream
what peace of mind
bison must have brought, rumbling
crescendo from beneath
a Blackfeet tepee camp on this very spot
in earshot of Ulm Pishkun
one-fifth of this millennium ago.

But my heart is more familiar with the wind
and so the clock's red embers flare
brighter with each gust—3:09, 3:10,
3:11, 3:11 and then
dark. It is time,
the religious warn us, to repent, no *stop*
button on Armageddon's alarm. Now,
the power dead—no coffee, heat, light
warming these words—I want seconds
back into my life. But they have been
kidnapped by this insidious wind
snipping the phone lines. It knows
I have no one to call on

but myself. Lurking in the same blackness
as unanswered prayers, it knows
my poems are not enough
to pay its large ransom
in small unmarked lives. It knows
and so it goes on rolling me
over and over in this tumbleweed sleep,
not one fenceline or dream in sight.

Equine Houdini

Medieval torture chamber grate of pipe
crosshatched with angle iron
spiked with ring-shanks to stringers
splintered over a bottomless borrow pit,
the cattle guard—unlikely armed to the teeth
by Rambo using blueprints
drafted by the Marquis de Sade
but anything's possible—could snap the metatarsals
off *Tyrannosaurus rex. Equus houdinus,*
the vet dubbed our 22-year-old mare
with a tube of Bute paste and booster
shot for tetanus. Instead of weeping
inside, I can joke now too: maybe some angel Pegasus
swooped down just in the nicker of time—
maybe eohippus himself
reincarnated as a chopper pilot
lowered the rescue sling to his comrade
floundering for toe-holds
in the blackness below.
                              Her coagulated blood,
matted with shredded flesh
and hair tufts, clung to rust-
pitted, serrated edges
for a rainless month after. It drew me
often to that thin break-of-day horizon crease
between fury and faint-heartedness
whenever I glimpsed where she'd wallowed
and likely whinnied into the dark
her shrill call to us far from home
on the one wrong night.
                              Does it matter why
I imagine a sorrel fox
with three paws? Ponder on how
the gate got unchained? Mull over the irony

behind our flying to Oklahoma City
to receive the bronze
horse and rider sculpture
award for a book titled *All This Way*
for the Short Ride? All that counts is
the mare's miraculous escape
with leg bones and tendons intact, still
carrying her, cock-prompt and in command,
to the galvanized feed tank she bangs her right
front hoof against, the most
melodious reveille to ever drum
me out of a sad bugled dream and on
my happy way to her haystack galley.

For Cody

Putting the Rodeo *Try* into Cowboy Poetry

Let's begin with the wildest landscape, space
inhabited by far more of them
than our own kind and, yes, we *are* talking
other hearts, other stars. Fall in love with all
that is new born—universe, seedling, dawn,
human, foal, calf. Love equally
the seasons, know each sky has meaning,
winter-out the big lonesomes, the endless
horizons our hopes sink beyond
once every minute, sometimes
seeming never to rise
again for air or light,
for life. Fall *madly* in love
with earth's fickle ways. Heed
hard the cosmos cues, the most
minuscule pulsings, subtle nods—no heavy-
handed tap or poke, nothing muscular,
no near-death truths revealed, no telephone
or siren screaming us out of sleep
at 3 a.m. Forget revelation.
Forgive religion. Let's believe instead in song
birds or Pegasus, the only angels
we'll ever need. Erase for good
inspiration from our Random *Bunk-*
House Dictionaries, from our petty heads
and pretty ambitions. Poetry is not
the grace or blessing we pray for—Poetry
is the Goddess for whom
we croon. Sing and surely we shall see
how she loves our music in any key—
any color, any creed, any race, any breed. Rhyme
if the muse or mood moves us
to do so. Go slow. Walk
then trot, lope then rock

and roll for even a split second, our souls
in the thundergust middle, the whole
world suddenly *getting western,*
pitching a tizzy fit, our horses
come uncorked—just as we were
seriously beginning to think
we savvied the salty? To believe we could
ever turn this stampede,
like steers, into a milling
circle? Into a civil gathering of words?

In Memory of Buck Ramsey

Living in Snake Country

First the barber sickling fuzz
around the mole, electric clippers
cool and heavy
against my neck. Then the rattler moved
like mercury or birdshot
in a camouflaged sleeve, thick muscle
mounted on a mechanical track
of vertebrae—the fuse lit, ballistic
missile sensors alerted to the pulse
of my horse, his shod hooves
stomping harder, closer.

Those clippers vibrated at the nape,
at nerves near the surface. I whipped
the heel-knot end of a lariat
at the snake slowly swallowed
by a gopher hole—found the blood-
stubbed tip of tail, a spear point,
ragged flesh clinging to the rattle
like petals of Indian paintbrush.

Back at the round corral, I shook
the remnant cupped between my palms,
shook the muffled maraca and danced
and sang *La Cucaracha* to the dog
who cowered at my antics. Shamed,
I sat thinking on a high rail
how the quick strike will throb
with each swelling step toward my knowing
what nicked me on the shin
was not a willow stick
tripped loose beneath my boot:

maybe while I'm traipsing knee-deep in meadow
fescue, mustard, clover and brome

on a horsefly July morning. Or maybe
brisket-deep in the wild hay and mint
along the crick, winding my way,
lured toward a favorite pool
near the missile silo—one step too close
to a silence of my own making.

The Day the War Began

I fed the dog and he was glad,
a bald eagle lit in the red
willows ignited
by a sinking winter sun, and prairie
chickens swept low in squadrons
over the hay meadow. Wind swirled
through glacial upthrust country, around
the nosecone rock named Haystack Butte,
old snow smoldering
during countdown. I breathed hard
toting haybales and grain
to the horses, to a field mouse
trapped in the slick tin feeder. Undaunted,
it sat on its haunches and lifted,
with deft fingers, a single
rolled kernel of corn
and ate in the warmth
inches from the filly's nostril. Three
lone coyotes on a trio of knolls
stopped me cold in the center
of a triangle of cry. They called to mind
the Hopi, their ancient tablet
warning of this war. East of here,
a crow-flown mile, the missile silo
lights, powered as always by the right
darkness, flickered on—less innocuous
in the dusk of that day. I forgot
I'd already fed the dog
licking his bowl clean a second time
within the war's first hour—so lovely,
the oblivion of another world
where instinct says, this simply, *live on.*

*For Joel Nelson, Rod McQueary
and Bill Jones*

Old Sorrel Mare Turning More and More Roan

She would not have stood still for this
just a year ago, at 24, without halter—
the Bute paste syringe I ease between her lips
twice a day, arm draped around her drooping neck,
our eyes, a few inches apart, hers
crusty and, lately, seeping
as I come closer each evening
to believing the ultimate
meaning of life is nothing
more than accepting death. I kiss her brow
at dawn, lick a fingertip, rub away
the crud beneath her eyes, scratch
her sagged belly, say *good morning ol' girl,*
feed her the healthiest-looking flakes,
walk spryly back to the house,
pour hot coffee atop the half-cup of lukewarm,
phone my 81-year-old Mother. I kiss again
the old mare's brow at dusk,
massage her belly, enjoy watching her head poised
young-colt-high, noble as she held it
in her foaling days. I fork her the greenest
leafiest alfalfa-brome mix,
plod the shadowy path
back to the house—so much longer
now, in the echo of my own *goodnight,* knowing
I have already phoned home.

Feeding the Creatures I Used to Eat

Long-stemmed roses, slow romantic kiss, sweet
dark chocolates in heart-shaped boxes,
Hallmark cards we call *valentines*
mean nothing to cottontails and prairie chickens
hunched, headless and mottled,
motionless as cantaloupes
in a minus 25 February 14th dawn
outside my kitchen window. They are waiting,
I am finally free enough to believe, for me
to flail, fistful after fistful,
their daily pail of grain. Each golden toss aloft
peppers the sheet of fresh snow
like lead shotgunned into freezer wrap
to test-pattern the deadliness
of the full choke's spread. How many
lovers today will consummate love
with sumptuous meals of flesh
turned euphemistically into *New York strips,*
medallions, chateaubriand, provençale, fine
cuisine long after the last loving drop
drips from the jugular. Guilt, sentiment, intimacy—
bone, blood, muscle—is what moves me,
still in slippers and shirt sleeves,
before coffee, juice, oatmeal and toast,
through the porch door—one step,
one breath, one hundred degrees colder. Stricken
instantaneously naked as Cupid
pink and unarmed in this flurry of birds,
this scamper of rabbits, this quiver
of little red hearts, I am wild, alive, in love.

Tender

What I would gladly give in silver
certificate minutes, or gold
hour tokens, to truly believe,
falsely or not, that the animal brethren
in our families—living never long enough,
turning old and ill
three, five, seven times
faster than we do—understand
when we cannot
do anything more
to keep them with us. I would trade
bullion from my own soul's trove, cash-in
an armored heart full—
every brick, ingot, locked canvas bag
I could get my bandit hands on
and lift, no matter that it means
I am not here now
writing this, that it means I could
not witness the old mare, Cody,
knowing why and forgiving
the sad man, looking at the ground,
walking so slowly toward her one morning
way too early with her pail of grain.

Tracks

Outside my picture window, a jack rabbit
stakes his claim to the brush
I stacked last fall for winter burning.
Circling his thatched hut of cottonwood limbs,
the loop he's made in new snow
looks like the imprint of an 8-plait
lariat a cowboy laid
around his camp in desert sand
to fence off rattlers.

During boyhood autumns, snowshoe rabbits turning
white before first snow, I'd climb
the backs of brush piles
heaped all summer to Uncle Hank and Dad
logging their hardwood forties
with horses. I'd bounce on bowed legs—
feet set in the forks of branches—standing
ahorseback like a trick rider,
or a silver screen cowboy hero
leaping from singletree to singletree
to retrieve the reins of a runaway
six-hitch stage. Riding full gallop,
I'd flush for Uncle and Dad
a trapshoot of panicked rabbits
and revel in the smell of the gunpowder West.

The rest of my life I spent loving
the hunt, until I caught myself
grieving over a lop-eared pet,
Hopalong, who died in my arms
without the Hollywood romance
of a heart-shot partner. Today, my father
snowshoes into his forty with feed
for the animals he names

as once he named each gun
mothballed now in cubbyholes
of the hunting shack. He's learned
how we suffer double when lives we take
come back. Under a jacklight moon,
tonight I'll set a circle of carrots,
root tips upright, vigil wicks
flickering from snowdrifts
around my house. The rabbit's braided track,
should morning bring magic and luck,
will figure-8 his home with mine,
keeping us both safe from snake and flame.

3

I BELIEVE

The poem, the song, the picture
is only water drawn from
the well of the people,
and it should be given back to them
in a cup of beauty
so that they may drink,
and in drinking
understand themselves.

— Frederico Garcia Lorca

I Believe

I have lived other lives, maybe the most
recent, and most often, as a woman
stalked throughout time. I am convinced
I have been a black man
branded by a master on his plantation—
shackled, lashed. Or was I an animal,
say a zebra or giraffe, a trophy
elephant, rare parrot, silverback gorilla,
some herbivore or, perhaps
likelier so, a combat soldier
hunkered on a moonless night in jungle
suddenly still. I believe I have been
the hunted, prey to a predator
whose life did not at all rest
upon my dying. I believe I will live
other lives, pray one of them will not end
on scarlet notes of fear, breathless
victim counting down from five
to the last heartbeat, the boa constrictor
pit of quicksand swallowing harder—lips
going under first, then earholes, nostrils, eyes,
arms stretched toward merciful God, fingertips touching
the final light, the final light
touching back, touching
so helplessly
back.

Shoes

What atrocities befell my Slavic ancestors
during the war, I cannot say. But I've heard
Czeslaw Milosz read poems in Polish
from the pulpit of Washington D.C.'s Church
of the Reformation. His words, at once familiar
and gorgeously foreign to my ear, were kin
to our cowboy verses lilting
through the Library of Congress
the night before. The morning after
hearing Milosz, I wept
different tears in the Holocaust Museum,
one for each mildewed shoe
heaped in a musky, dark exhibit
backdropped by large snapshots of mountains
of shoes at Auschwitz. Brogan or slipper
resting upright, did those, open to the sky,
signal to the ashes of feet
drifting from the stacks—brittle, warm
flakes of flesh finding their way
defiantly back to their shoes? I am torn for life
between the desperate need to believe
in the unfathomable, and the grimace
to forget—what I smelled, what I tasted,
what I heard and witnessed, but could not
reach out and caress. I wanted to run
my cupped hand into each shoe with hope
of finding one matched pair
still together five decades after
the condemned grandmother's, grandfather's,
husband's, wife's, sister's, brother's,
daughter's, son's, cold numb fingers crawled
through their last unlacings.
                              Milosz's poems
spoke to 83 years of knowing how death
fills up a life—the suddenness of manhood and then
back to a boy reliving his fancy
for fiery workings of the village
blacksmith hammering out iron shoes

in a Lithuanian livery. Cowboy poetry, I swear,
pinged from pulpit to pews
to choir loft and cathedral ceiling
in D.C. that night. I wore sneakers out of fear
for dark city corners and hatred still
seething in the ethnocentric minds of man,
left my hat and boots in the room
and walked, bewildered in squared-off circles,
after seeing Museum and Milosz. Avoiding the faces
of everyone I passed, left me alone
in my world of shoes—leather, laces, tongues,
toes, heels, seams and eyes
of trainload upon trainload of the doomed
peeking between slats of boxcars—the coldest
exhibit you'll ever step into—where they stood
still in their shoes.
                    What I ask now is
that each of this world's soldiering poets writes life
back into one shoe of the persecuted—softly
as a mother's fingertip to her teething child's gums,
rub olive oil into the leather until you feel it
breathing again. Choose your most truthful
words, your most vital music,
worthy of being sung in synagogues, in temples,
in kivas and tepees, museums and mausoleums
and in the very church where Milosz sang,
where a woman, moved to tears
by the otherworldliness of such singing,
handed up to him a single rose—his final lines
like the Gods' own chain lightning
dancing across a thousand hands
lifted in long applause. As I watched
the shaking mosaics of stained glass
windows arched above me, I feared this poem
would make its way closer to home. Now, I must
sing to you of the bugle-
beaded horse-tracks-on-buckskin
Sioux moccasin, so tiny against the black
mountains of shoes—one baby's bootee found
frozen in the snow at Wounded Knee.

Angelina, My Noni's Name, Means *Messenger*

All the flesh I saw was the beggar's palm
circled by sunlight. The hand,
beckoning out of the black serape,
looked like one I knew the pulse of
as a child, guided before first light
to mass. She wore cotton stockings—
her legs folded to one side
on the red cobble where she sat—
and terra-cotta-colored rubber rings of Mason jars,
the same garters my Noni wore. Three decades
past her death, what draws me at dawn
toward the cathedral in Morelia, in Mexico,
must be the carillon
settling into the pink stone
courtyard of the inn—a trembling
that climbs the arcades, that pools
with fountain burble and lures me like purple
finches' chirm amid the bougainvillea.

My steps into the nave become altar-boy
pious beneath murals domed toward infinity, beneath
the pipe organ, two stories high, beneath melting
sanctuary of gold baroque. Dwarfed
by graphic Spanish *Cristos,* I consider each
breath, one indulgence prayed-for years ago
in this candlewax air. Something familiar
murmurs through the church—Noni's Italian
litanies recited near the rood. Stooped,
the ancient priest shuffles an inch per step
from his confessional, young boys kneeling
to kiss his ring—one of them rises, turns back, touches
his cassock like a relic. This sudden chill
is not the return of childhood fear, but faith,
that force of flesh and blood
always reaching out—my first communion
glimpse into the chalice filled with Hosts,
the pesos' radiance in Noni's palm.

Tsankawi

We walk where the Anasazi danced
on the tablerock above their cropland,
a baby rattler, licorice-tongued,
sunning, and the sun-bellied horny toad,
camouflaged and crouched—
its mouth circling its head,
an old man's scowl strained
toward a smile—and the widow spinning
web around a cricket
kicking free but for one
tether stretching to hold against the violent
spasms of a snared hind leg.

And the cone of the piñon tree,
a green fist opening
finger by finger, like a child letting go
of something sticky—the brown-
shelled seeds, iridescent,
falling finally free. On hands and knees,
we pick them out of needled duff
beneath a tree centuries old,
nibble their sweet ivory meat
all afternoon, as we amble through the caves
of cliff dwellers, along their paths—
finger- and toe-holds worn in sandstone and basalt—

amid the glint of potsherds,
glimpse of Mimbres designs painted
with yucca brushes, amid jagged lightning spear,
spiral, coiled snake, and flute player
petroglyphs. Omniscient-looking,
one figure, seeming to wave good-bye
to the raw age of rock, sun, water,
reminds us of all things cyclic

and simple—the stickman's hand raised
in a breeze of thin green lizards
across obsidian face, as if to whisper
see you again, in some same time, soon.

For Jack Loeffler and Ed Abbey

On My Birthday, The Serpent—

disturbed from his moist coiled sleep in the cool
humus beneath the horse trough
triveted an inch off the ground
by mildewed boards—glides
between my feet. It has been
startled by water
hose thrashing the roof
over its head, brass nozzle
striking side-to-side
wildly under the sudden thrust—spigot
handle yanked up full.
                                        I rocket 4 feet
vertical on my 48th, my bull
hide boots hovering—*I'll be*
go-to-hell!—above the bull snake's only lane
of escape. Pole bean tendril reaching
sinuously for the invisible
fingers of light, the snake arches
an s-curved third of itself
toward May 25th first rays—both our skins
absorbing the morning
more yellow than green.
                                        We are bewildered
in the midst of this birth, this quick
perpendicular coming
together. The snake swirls
its shimmering way into the shade
beneath the horse trailer, wraps
its umbilical self back up in ribbons
of grass—the earthly gift
unscripted, unscrolled,
unpossessed, always at first
a touch tougher to love.

How the Beluga Spoons

For a whispered secret or to steal a kiss, I lean out
over her tank, like a longship's figurehead,
far as a man in love dare reach
without altogether letting go. My fingers grip the rail
behind me, arms contorted to flippers. Rippling
in this aquamarine mirror, a human face
becomes the face of a whale
nosing cautiously through
the surface, that crystalline plane
between two worlds. I smile, her lips opening
into her eye-to-eye cavern. I throw a kiss, toss it
gently with a nod. She dips her lower jaw,
scoops it full as a waterwheel bucket,
and with a gesture, rightly larger,
wetter, more deliberate than mine,
approves our courtship. She chortles
my comic response, my straightman nonchalance,
ladles another mandible full, and showers me
again with kisses. By this passage, we vow
to the cosmos a romance revived
from eons of dormancy. We feel our way,
sonar and sight, slowly
into the gray swales—lovers
sounding our one laughter
wave after wave, quasar to quasar,
toward that first rollicking spark and whatever
leviathan god brought it on.

To Gerald Fuentes—May Heaven Swoon for Him Her Handsomest Storybook Bevy

On a planet we've poxed with the beauty
of ourselves, it's a walk through the toxic park
picking from front page news alone
our recommended daily dose
of heartbreak. Jaded, immunized against
sentimental tetanus and melodrama—
my emotions pumped full of cold Demerol—I read
the newspaper like a patron of a greasy spoon
for three-plus decades opens the same
laminated hashbrown-Tabasco-burger-stained menu
minus all false hope. Today, page two
allots an obvious, large block of space
to a *before*, but not *after*, photograph
of Gerald Fuentes, from Pacullpa, Peru,
who does not strain, it seems, posing
the closest he can to a picturebook
little boy's smile through his cockeyed
cattywampus face. Nose flattened
cheek-to-cheek, eyes spanned
almost around the corners of his forehead, his grin
literally ear-to-ear, no way
could our glitzed and glittered, smoked
and, worst of all, mirrored world
tag him *normal. Seven-year-old Gerald Fuentes
wanted to be handsome*, the first line reads,
and have a girlfriend. He died without one
little glimpse of the new face
surgeons, revising nature
gone awry, cut and pasted,
to make him pretty. Why do we need this
sad news revisited, my tiny reminder of one
life coming so close
to knowing the miraculous
happy ending almost man-made? Because I can

not deliver us all
framed glossies of this page two
Tribune picture to hang on our walls
of misshapen angels. Gerald Fuentes left earth
not one cosmetic scar, only the perfect
curvature of his artistic kiss
brush-stroking each nurse's cheek, a heart-
broken surgical world
filled with his girlfriends.

Montana Second Hand

Down's syndrome can't hinder the Saint
Vincent de Paul thrift store
troubadour of the shoe department,
John Jasmann, singing his pedal steel guitar
love songs into his rhapsodical
job—sorting used footwear
into rows from his shopping cart piled
high with each day's fresh stock. His photo
album propped open
in the child carrier, Polaroids
showcasing him at work—and his touch
of personal panache, one flashy cravat hanging,
half-hitched, from the cart's push-bar—
he belts out a line of Louisiana Hayride
classic, ...*son of a gun*
we'll have big fun on the bayou.
                                Hank Williams
lilting hit after hit, John
presses his palms to the Walkman headphones,
as if holding a lover in a long kiss,
and takes wing on the Nashville airwaves
bringing us a little ...*how's about cookin'*
somethin' up with me.
                        Strange as this may sound,
John stumbled once onto the key of C,
his usual out-of-tune
cacophony turning
suddenly to a melodic
lovely a cappella: *I'm so lo-o-nesome*
Iiii could cryyy.
                        Listen—as each shopper,
gawking with awe toward *Shoes,*
pictures some rockabilly god,
some rhythm-'n'-blues aficionado,

maybe Saint Vinny himself,
rolling a ruby-ringed finger
over the solid gold dial
tuned to *Angelic Debut*.
                              May grace taking shape
tangibly in a single line of singing
draw us all one lonesome day
toward the mysterious
display of white shoes
staggered with black boots
across wrought iron racks. There, may each shelf
holding the notes, sharps, flats,
show us how the maestro—excited
by the infinite, cued to the unique
movements we make
arranged together in perfect time—writes
out of all our used lives
one sweet music.

                    For John Jasmann, brother Mark,
                    and Vicky Howell

Imperfect Strangers

Friday night at the Club Cigar, smoke-
filled box of ruckus, office workers
blowing off the week's pent-up steam,
peanut-uprising peanut-shell debris
littering the floor—innocuous
symbolic flipping-off of bosses,
jobs they'd like to eighty-six
from their lives forever, if only
their lotto numbers would appear in time
to preclude their obituaries
in the Great Falls Tribune—here,
amid the hodgepodge of us
old hippies turned middle-aged yupsters,
sits a Montana throwback throwaway,
Delphin Smith, all by himself
on his 57th birthday he desperately wants someone
to know about. The only cowboy
hat in the joint, I'm his logical choice,
his one hope, I understand way too late,
as he stares me down, grins
his jack-o'-lantern grin I catch
surprisingly through the still-sharp corner
of my younger-day barhopping eye. I sense
Delphin is not one of those fighters
figuring he's still good
for as many bar brawls as he has
front teeth—2, maybe 3—
left in his head. Words come hard
as he leans a working man's thick scarred paw
on the edge of our rickety table, our beer
glasses sloshing over their rims, him
slipping his birth certificate
out of a pearl-snapped shirt pocket—flashing
it, as if it *were* that jackpot-winning ticket,

then setting it into the spilled-beer-
peanut-husk slop while begging us
to quiz him about anything, names, places, dates,
worn away and faded to nothing, his life's
most critical criteria, no more
or less indelible than anyone's, all of ours
on the same sad wane. We humor him a bit,
ask for our tab, assure the waitress
that *Delphin J. Smith, born September 29, 1943*
to Rosetta, the rest too smeared to read, is not
why we are leaving. We have reservations
at the Italian restaurant down the block
where minutes later we are seated
at a sidewalk window. Scarfing down our calamari
appetizer with crusty bread
sopped in olive oil and balsamic—lit
candles flickering off long-stemmed glasses
of Chianti as we celebrate nothing
special in our own lives—we regret not
buying a birthday beer for Delphin
walking by outside, just a heart's-beat, an arm's-reach
through thin curtain and glass,
away from our table into his one big night alone.

Manners

On a morning when your northern breath smokes
you shake hands with the weathered
old rancher wearing gloves. They hold
what little heat his bones still stoke,
cushion the vicious bite
of rheumatoid arthritis. Boisterous
greeting billowing
into a huge plume, your blue steel-jawed paw
gets the quick-draw drop on him. You are not
yet seasoned enough to know pain's drumroll
rousting you long before dawn
seven days a week, the same cadence
he is lucky to work or walk off
by dusk. Yellow and red cotton,
his chore glove cocoons your hand
in a warmth that flashes you
back to thick wool
mittens your mother knitted. Didn't they soothe
you beautifully until cruel puberty
bamboozled you into becoming cool,
into swapping *soft* for *macho?* His soft words,
delivered almost invisibly,
barely a wisp of steam behind them,
surprise you. *Excuse the glove,*
he declares with the air of a knight
still in armor after his long ride
home. You nod without knowing
what you are bowing to
is wisdom, the lyrical kinship of skin
against skin, two hands together in one
clasp of applause and nothing but
hard work's firm grip on silence in between.

The Hand

In South Africa, a white aristocrat grabs
the hand of an elderly black man
sitting in the dirt on the edge
of a lush crop. The white man
picks the black man's hand up
as if it were a self-serve gasoline nozzle,
pulls it toward a reporter
and mechanically squeezes the wrist
to spread wide the thick callused fingers
and palm. The white man holds his own hand
open side by side. *Do you see
the difference? he asks. What
does his hand look like to you? How
can you say we are the same?*

Do you see the difference? he asks again,
the reporter stunned by what he is hearing,
while the black man sits inanimate,
his working cowboy hand
filling the camera's close-up lens
with a landscape of canyons,
coulees and arroyos, buttes and mesas, mountains
and plains the black man might have ridden,
hands shaped by pistol grip, lariat, and reins,
had he been born of another geography
and time—just another wind-burned hand
of a *cavvy* man, sinew and knuckle,
flesh and blood, pocked, porous, scarred,
and dark as lathered latigo. The hand
alongside the aristocrat's
tissue-paper appendage always reaching to take
even another man's hand, and own it,
and hold it open, because he knows the fist
is as big as a man's heart
and *this* is the difference he fears.

For Alan Thompson and Frank Phillips

Pathetic Fallacy

They have put to death the most elderly
male grizzly bear ever trapped
in Montana. After 28 seasons
rot his teeth, but not his will
to go on feeding, he ransacks cabins
on the Flathead—a homeless man
chancing upon paper bags
of what he hopes is food
or some other warmth abandoned
on the street.
                    Finders, keepers,
I say, in this helter-skelter West
where we feed, clothe, shelter, humor
the satanic predator—not worth naming—
decades after a slaughter
that nothing we should ever classify as *plant,*
animal or *rock,* let alone *human,*
should ever be capable of.
                              On our off-kilter scales
of unpoetic justice, we weigh
28 years of noble heartbeat
against 16 unoccupied cabins—innocent victims
minding their own business
beneath righteous skies?
                    The Great Oz
has spoken and goes on, as fraud, speaking
in the name of whatever agency rules
whatever fairytalish foofaraw is these days
licensing the executioner. It's every bit as easy
reducing paragons of wildness
to pariahs, as it is vilifying the poet
as anarchist or rogue.
                    After reading what seems
my own obituary in the Great Falls Tribune,

I dream the bear, not so *horribilis* at all
rattling the latch of my back door,
wakes me out of dreams too sweet,
cautions me to curb the sugar, to be careful
what I eat before bedtime.
                              I'm ready now.
I refuse to hibernate in silence.
Come and get me. Trailer to my portal
your foolish-looking culvert, your so-called *live
trap* no poet worth his clawed notebooks
could ever be duped by. The rhetoric you use
as bait stinks. I don't give a shit
about your scientific research
or reasoning. The mad poet waits
with pencils honed, erasers gnawed,
my stomach growling.

Wolf Tracks on the Welcome Mat

But in the ruckus, in the whirl,
We were the wolves of all the world.

—Buck Ramsey

Long after dark, the big bad black
wolf, winded, knocks his softest
dewclawed knock on my straw door. He begs,
far too proud for handouts, a heart-
to-heart. Although a love poem is right
in the middle of whispering sweet
naughty nothings to me
as we stroll arm-in-arm
across the page, I ask him in,
fix him a thick ham steak and eggs,
Charles M. Russell's favorite.
                              The wolf
wants to pay me 7 million dollars for my trouble,
for the first home-cooked meal
he's eaten in eighty years,
but his pockets are empty
as a cowboy poet's pockets
the morning after drawing his pay
for Saturday night's show. Thus, the wolf
breaks into his rendition of *Moanin'*
At Midnight, a blues song so haunting,
so harmonious with the whole
toe-tapping cosmos keeping tempo,
it makes my guard hairs
bristle—silver needles tweaked
into each pore, the master
acupuncturist knowing exactly where
pain blazes its steepest trails.
                              The wolf circles
back to old Montana

as we go back to our childhood
homeground decades later to mourn
our own passing. We all crave, admit it,
what's vaguely familiar, the distant
glimpse of wild beginnings. We are all hungry.
We are happy. We all hurt and howl
louder the second time around
because we hope to learn to love our own
howling, as we love our healing—
all of us, from the same packed stage,
singing for our suppers.

For Hank Fischer

4

ANTIPASTO!

*And if contemporary poetry needs to get more
serious about anything, it is pleasure.*

— Dana Gioia

*Bring to poetry the passion that goes into politics
or buying a piece of meat.*

— Theodore Roethke

I'm just a public entertainer who has understood his time.

— Pablo Picasso

Antipasto!

The tongue loves Antipasto! The linguini way
each button-mushroom syllable—gold
nubbin plucked from hardwood stump—lingers
toward the uvula, palate to lips
to palate. Say, *floret,* Slowly
say, *ivory cauliflower floret. Min-i-a-ture
sweet pickle. Red bell pepper. Chickpea.*
Say, *celery heart, albacore fillet,
pearl onion.* And say, *ebony olive*—
that favorite we fought over
as kids. Only the grade A
make Mom's cut to this concertino
of sauce—tomato, virgin olive oil, herbs—
put-up in pints, the red-orange
pantry rows. Say, *Antipasto!*
Pass the Antipasto! Thrill the inner ear
to this belfry of syllables, churchbell
meals festive enough for triple table leaves,
for old-country crystal
chiming Chianti salutes to family,
to Mom—*good health!*—for Antipasto!

For my brothers, Mark and Gary

Bringing Home the Poems

Born into a Polish-Italian immigrant clan
of hunter-gatherers, garlic and tomato tenders,
wood-burners, preserve putter-uppers, whiskey
distillers and maker-from-scratch
curers and procurers, I have picked,
caught, shot, cut, piled, wrapped,
canned all my life and, thus, have become a writer
of poems. *Just try to think of these*
jagged-on-the-right hearty packagings—
I urge my folks, now that I've learned
to choose, like mushrooms over toadstools,
only the edible metaphor—*as something wild,*
something to fill up your bucket with,
haul home, float the twigs and bugs out of, and boil
down into sweet renderings
you'll pull from the shelf like warm, fresh déjà vu
seven months into another midwest winter.
                                        Okay, okay,
let's forget I ever said déjà vu. Would it help,
I wonder, if I plucked these lines myself,
letter by plump ripe letter,
handful after handful of firm syllables,
off the pages, if I processed my words first
in quart jars, or cold-packed them in cider
vinegar, salt, and dried red chile pods
like Pete Lombardo's hot garlic dills—if I
stacked them, by the rick or cord,
in nice even tiers alongside ash,
oak, maple, birch, or double-wrapped them
labeled with wax pen
for the freezer? Then, would it be easier
to explain to the neighbors what it is
I do to bring home the prosciutto,
without saying *poet*? *I know, Dad—may as well*

tell them I sell fish to Mafia hitmen.

From Chicago,
I puddle-jump into muskie country,
fight two fifty-pound Samsonites
bricked full of books nobody bought
after my reading. When I show off the lunker
check they paid me for the gig, *Remember,*
Mom says, *the real job you had once*
picking nightcrawlers for a dime a dozen? Tonight
Dad and I, in a light rain, will kneel
side by side again on mossy lawns
below streetlights, stretch a hundred dozen fat ones
from the earth into our Hills Brothers tins
squirming full, while Mom drapes linguini
noodles in three-foot-long strands
over broom-handle perches
between kitchen chairs. We'll pack, tomorrow,
the Samsonites with jars of jam, chowchow,
antipasto, with hard salami, dried pasta,
slabs of Asiago. I'll stack the poetry
next to kindergarten keepsakes in the attic—
my first A-through-Z letters
in a Big Chief tablet, the one book
my folks still review with raves,
the earliest words, like seeds, preserved.

For Karl Peschke

Potatoes

Unless they've been clandestinely launched whole
into orbit as a satellite welcome wagon
gunnysack toward alien good will,
unless I've been mispronouncing *sputnik*
all these years, the quartet of big reds
freshly forked from Dad's garden—
stowaways in my carry-on luggage
above our heads—might be the highest
flying spuds since Kitty Hawk. I do not believe
in happenstance, so when the strapping
young man in the window seat
insists on Close Encounters of the Third Kind
(note allusion here to mashed potato scene)
after I've already warned him *I'm a poet*
running on no sleep—a threat
that deters him not one tater tot iota—
touché, I think, as I buckle myself
in for the, unbeknownst to me at the time, starchy ride
and fire politely right back at the guy, *so*
*what is it **you** do?* As deadpanned
as the metal-detector deputy in bouffant
when I cautioned her not to nuke back into humus
the tubers I'm sending through her microwave,
he proclaims, with a bit of sinister
unwhispered boast to his tone, *I*
am a potato breeder. It's a good thing
I'm graced with greater control than you folks
listening to this true tale. I, at least, am able
to draw—with a dull molar, no less—
a Red Cross pint from my inside cheek,
to restrain my spasmodic bladder, to counter,
without a single twitch
of upper lip or brow, without one Adam's apple
bobble, *Ahhh, so you breed...*(long pause)

potatoes. Luckily, my celibate darlings, huddled
like the epitome of virgin innocence
in their brown paper sack, are out of earshot,
I think, until I hear, from above, a jumping bean raucous
guffaw over Fargo, en route to Great Falls,
Montana—thank God not that Sodom
and Gomorrah of spud-lust states,
Idaho. So this is how I learned every *in* and *out*
of the chipping business, and yes,
the skins, like livers, do absorb
pesticide and fertilizer residues, but not enough
to compel one to forfeit the roughage benefit,
unless the subcutaneous epidermic layer has turned
green and, therefore, toxic. Incidentally,
the scientific name, should you find yourselves
in future discussion with horticultural savants
is *Solanum tuberosum.* I drink 6 vodkas
on the rocks over Bismarck. You got your *Yukon
Golds,* your *Fingerlings* and *Yellow Finns,* your *Chieftains,*
your *Chippewas, Kennebecs, Burbank Russets, Early
Gems,* your *Colorado Longs* and *Pontiac Reds,*
you name it—this young fella has come eyebud-
to-Ph.D.-eyebud with every creed, color, race,
model, make, nationality and post-mortem
transmogrification. Me? I'm French-and curly-
fried by the time we touch down
at midnight in Montana and I say *buh-bye,
my little sweet potato pie,* to the stewardess
who refuses to return my perfectly rhymed *toodle-oo*
adieu—I'm scalloped, twice-baked, *platskied,* jo jo'd,
au gratined, shoestringed, mashed, colcannoned, vichyssoised,
hashbrowned and having green potato skin
hallucinogen flashbacks and, worse,
forecasts, as suddenly every Samsonite suitcase,
every garment bag, every nylon backpack
and canvas duffel transmutates, right before
my protuberant eyes, into bulbous burlap sacks

on the baggage carousel, where I stand—
the world's number one vegetable,
between Rod Serling and Stephen King—confused
and drooling, mesmerized by the big blue-
lettered logo stenciled to the front of every gunny:
          Zarzyski's Purple Mazurkas
            We Put the P-O-E-T in
            P O T A T O E S

For Christian Thill

Running On Empty

Say you are out there somewhere between
Ingomar and Enid, Kaycee and Meeteetse,
some big Montana-Wyoming open, the red
needle of your word gauge
flat on its flat face against **E**,
not even a death-throes last spasm or nerve-
quiver flinch, when your front tires hit frost-
heave tarred cracks on Poetry's hard
shoulderless washboard road. You switch over
to your reserve tank, cheer the needle
straining, straight-backed, off the mat,
a gymnast breaking barely by one rep the world
record push-up mark, elbows locked firm
at maybe an eighth of a tank. You believe
you'll make it on fumes to the muse's next
station, where you'll be very willing
to shell out however many simoleons
per poetic line it takes to fill
both tanks to their nickel-plated caps
with the highest creative octane
heart and soul and mind can buy,
regular unleaded be damned. You guzzle
thick black coffee by the gallon
washing down a pound of rare T-bone,
three eggs over real easy, blood and yolk
oozing together in a pool
lapping a spatula'd pile of hashbrowns
grilled crisp and slathered
in sausage gravy. You sop your platter
clean with butter-sponged sourdough
toast, tip the waitress a cool fin,
swagger back to your two-door Dick-Hugo
Buick convertible you punch from 0 to 80
as you siphon the sweet night

bouquet of rain-soaked sage into lobes
of your lungs spilling over. Dashboard lit,
that red-headed gymnast stretched out now on her back
against a grassy knoll and peering
up at the road map cosmos
with its jillion points of interest, not a single
solid or dotted line connecting any two, you,
running again on full, are itching
to cover ground, aching to fill-in
the loneliest blanks between
towns you mostly remember leaving
and go on loving only for their names.

For Jim Welch, Rick DeMarinis,
Quinton Duval, and Gary Thompson

Pheromones

Maybe it's the scent of the *MONTANA RANCH* brand
Tender Beef in Natural Juices
tin can filled with freshly sharpened number two
pencils—the pastoral jackfence
backlit by sunrise over the foothills
label—that attracts this box elder bug
to my writing desk every morning now
for the past three weeks. She (I'm sure) shows up
always late, an hour or so into the poem,
tiptoes over the oak, follows
the grain, like blazed trail,
to the edge of the notebook, then politely waits
until my pencil stills and lifts, her cue
to enter, her go-ahead signal to step
aboard and ride along with the unruly
words having their free-for-all ball,
today shaping UFO-esque
cryptic images and symbols into wheat
fields of blank pages. She traipses switchback
wakes of the freshest lead, catches
up with the poem, finally, after a long linebreak pause,
embraces with her forked antenna and 6 legs
the pencil. I launch it like a rocketship
slowly lifting off the pad,
add a soft *shhhhhhh* exhaust
sound-effect to enhance her drama,
lower the hovercraft to a foot-
high stack of books
perched near my chair. She waddles off,
naturally somewhat dizzy after her flight,
disappears into the black-ink-abyss
John Singer Sargent *Le Piano Noir*
jacket art of Billy Collins' *Sailing
Alone Around the Room.* I return

to find my words refusing to move
a single foot, to play on. They'll have nothing
further to do with the one they know
drove away their very first amorous fan—
right into the Venus flytrap
Casanova clutches of a far more notorious poet.

Bizarzyski—Mad Bard and Carpenter Savant
of Manchester, Montana—Feeds the Finicky Birds

Unlikely that my poems will ever land
in some *Norton Anthology of Ornithology*, let alone
The Guinness Bird Book of World Bon Appétit Records,
I want all you Audubon paesanos to hear right now
who's the first mad poet to ring-shank-spike
a fat, foot-long, freezer-burned muledeer salami
to the icy top of a railroad tie corner post
where I distract rambunctious flocks
of ravenous magpies squawking happily all winter
away from the purple finch/English sparrow
birdseed feeders. Maybe I'm first
also to have learned that even a scavenger clings
to certain proprieties and will
exercise its right to decline a handout. Once,
I placed a frozen block of tofu
atop the very same post. No way. Not one minuscule
peck. Like offering menudo, pâté, haggis
to a vegan. Poor tofu—it didn't even get
a second look, a quizzical magpie glance
of comical disgust or surprise. I did not know
these birds could smell, let alone whiff
tofu at 30 below. I've watched
them gobble-up a bloated road-killed polecat
for brunch under a blacktop-softening sun. And so
it sat there, through five chinooks, through spring
and summer, until the post, I suppose, osmosised it,
almost, along with that dangerous duo
of dago hitmen, Sal Monella and his sidekick, Bocci,
who must've thunk they'd bag a bird or two. But nothing
bit the dust, just like nothing bit the tofu. Thus,
I must confess—because I'm Catholic
and I'm unfulfilled unless I'm bearing guilt—
that I prayed very hard for scavenger forgiveness

as they laid their beady eyes upon my latest
feast and spiel: *My name is Paul. I'll be*
your server this winter. For your delight,
our hammered chef tonight has spiked,
in lieu of our usual alder-planked smoked salmon
on the menu, frozen chunk of venison
sopressa over creosoted post. It's free.
I'll be right back to take your order.

The Tumbleweed Munchies

After my nemesis, the stiff wind, howls,
under cover of darkness, *CHARGE!*
to her spiny urchin army of The Big Dry,
I find the scabrous bastards at first light
Velcroed by the battalion bunches
to every fenceline, shelterbelt, fissure, niche
of my choreful, not cheerful, life. *They might
have me surrounded, alrighty,* I think,
wringing my hands, laughing my demonic laugh,
but I have THEM cornered. I have
their roly-poly bouncy little backsides flattened
up against the wall. With my American Gothic
pitchfork held in bayonet stance, I thrust and tear
them away from their comrades,
stuff the spring-loaded cannon-fodder
sonsabitches into the 55-gallon burn barrel
coughing, choking, belching its thick brown
locomotive smoke until, POOF!—*Fee-Fry-
Foe* (especially *Foe*)-*Fum*—it whooshes, then rumbles
with incendiary delight. Romping
around the crematorium, I begin to love
the last scratchings of their tumbleweed toe-
nails down the inside walls of the drum. I savor,
more and more, each intoxicatingly hot
peekaboo into their scanty ashen remains
glowering back up at me from the pulsing red
tuba's fumarole wherein this basso profundo
musical disintegration takes place. I can't wait
to ramrod the next forkful into the black
maw *making my day* every couple minutes,
cannabis-esque aromas hovering in the dusk,
as if Beelzebub, his far-out groovy self,
had rolled the mother of all doobies
in Tumbleweed Hell, where I find myself

suddenly in a dead calm, smelling of hemp,
singed bald across both brows
and stricken with the inexplicable
severe craving for watercress tempura, fondued
baby squid, extra-extra-crisp, each bite
sizzling before my eyes upon the tines.

Cowboys & Indians

When my father does not *ride in* on time
for supper, I track him down,
find him wounded, fevered,
slumped on his big hairy Ernest
Borgnine forearms over his work bench
in the shop across the yard. Quivering,
sweat soaked through both his shirts,
he twists and torques
with needle-nose pliers in one fist
treble hooks of a Heddon Torpedo
run deep into the forefinger
of the other, bleeding
like a northern pike
gaffed through the gills.
                    He is the victim
of television westerns we watched
together every Saturday—Hoppy,
Widmark, Cooper, Fonda, Mix,
as cowboy or cavalry scout
in that patented scene where he
tortuously forces
the Arapaho, Comanche, Chiricahua, Shoshoni,
Sioux arrow he's been skewered by
all the way through his shoulder, snaps
the point off and then—to melodramatic
orchestral crescendo—pulls the slick
shaft back through
cleanly.
            Clearly, my pop has forgotten how
they'd all pass out cold, more than
a little to do, perhaps, with redeye
gizzard juice they'd guzzle,
save for that last antiseptic splash
spilled into the wound,

not to mention the ever-present
partner or sidekick, ever-ready
to cauterize—Bowie knife
agleam in the campfire's writhing
flame, in the moonlight's blaze. *DAD!*
I scream in lieu of puking,
Who in the heck do you think you are? Wild Bill
Polack?
      The surgeon, shaking
his noggin in Doc-Adams-of-Gunsmoke disgust,
works a fishing-leader-like, looped
wire gizmo to back the barbs
my father drove bone-deep
eventually out. *Lucky for us, hey Dad,*
I quip, driving home from Emergency—*lucky*
they didn't pack extractors like that
back in the old West? He grins
and I, together with him
again in front of our '50s Zenith TV,
gaze at the legendary
reflected in the windshield—big screen
cowboy hero he will always be.

For Anne and Richard Widmark

Cedarville Sweet

Cautious not to buck the cowboy code,
we salivate for weeks
before unsealing the gift we vowed to save
until Christmas, before slathering
impasto layers over our heavy-grained morning
toast. We raise our slices high,
salute John and Linda Hussa,
take the first bites, close our eyes
to the tastebud stampede
jubilating through the gray
coulees of our wintry brainpans. Stirring up
Surprise Valley—horse-'n'-cattle country—
California, this limb-bending
unruly, almost hallucinogenic, fruit
dances warmly into panoramic view
on the snowy screen of our one Montana
state of mind. Bedazzled, I flash
back to Linda's mischievous grin
as she teasingly lifts
this jar of crimson elixir,
inch-by-rich-red-inch, from the deep
pocket of her Carhartt
coat reading like a decade-long
tally of weather and work. She whiffs
one crested wheat grass seed hull,
a piece of twig, short faded-orange
filaments of nylon baling twine, sorrel
horse hairs off the lid. With a long breath,
she fogs the golden top, buffs
off the smudges with her sleeve,
counterclockwise, round and round and
hypnotically round until
finally holding it out with both hands
toward spellbound me. Oh, how those two
indelible words printed on the lid

WILD PLUM
sing of poetry, sing of friendship,
you can't help but spoon
so thick you have to sip its dripping
juices first—autumn desert sunset
runneling off the western edges of your spread.

Great Harvest Bread, Rock-'n'-Roll-'n'-God

Peace and love on a child's wintry earth
was simply a line of the Lord's
Prayer come real—a three-inch-thick
heel of peasant bread steaming beneath
white see-through butter
shavings melting
like last patches of icy snow
on a late-May afternoon. In January,
oven door of the Monarch stove open,
I sat with Noni on the woodbox,
ate fresh-baked Italian bread, tapped our toes
to Saturday polkas from the Philco. We laughed
at the lyrics *you can have her, I don't want her,*
she's too fat for me and the tabby
kitten batting a ball of cotton
string Noni rolled for years
from butcher-wrapped packages of Asiago
cheese, the closest thing to meat
she could afford, a quarter's worth
each week from Martini's display case.

                                    Give us
this day our daily bread, I prayed with her
at 6 a.m. mass without once thinking
God's body. I believed I could hear the yeast
breathing gently ten blocks from the church
through the most raucous blizzard. Before we stomped
and broomed snow off our boots back home,
blossoming loaves on steel sheets
slid into the oven with a sizzle of ice
crystals off Noni's mittens,
the kitchen filling with my very own
tangible fragrance of sanctifying grace.

                                    Guided back,
through thirty religionless years

toward my most sacred days, by the Great Harvest
Bakery's red neon behind steamed glass
at dawn, I am drawn to the godliness
of round squat loaves—profoundness of flour,
freedom of yeast, simplicity of water—
risen to the Woodstock rock of Country
Joe and the Fish, to Creedence Clearwater Revival,
The Stones, Deep Purple and Cream
keeping moon-filled eyes
in time with heels of hands kneading
something divine into the dough. Given the warmth
brought on by these bakers always smiling,
given a glass of Noni's homemade dago red
wine with a wedge of hard sharp cheese
on the side, given real butter
from loving people, I believe again
I can live alone on fresh-baked bread
but never on bread baked alone.

For Pete and Melané and all
the Great Harvest Flour Children

Sister Sundays

On the same morning I stoned to death
and drove over the prairie rattler
relaxed and sunning—as if something thick and sweet
slavered onto the warm gravel
near our fishing bridge where you creeled
two blue-ribbon brookies we sautéed
in chardonnay, dark olive oil, butter and chives
for Sunday brunch—we huckleberried
high in the rockies, a pair of pine squirrels
we pegged as lovers, eyeing our purple
fingertips feeling beneath
canopies of leaves for the fruit,
firm and erotic and urging
each bush toward earth. That same afternoon
we picked our buckets full, I bartered poetry
recited to the Hutterites
for pickling cukes from their horn-of-plenty
gardens on our way home from the mountains
and back over the bridge
where I stopped to cut the 8-tiered tail-tip off
the snake already crisp
in the dry heat. On the same dreamy evening of that
hunter-gatherer sabbath of the rattler,
of huckleberries we sampled
sweetened with pure maple syrup
over gourmet ice cream, orange flambéed sunset
through kitchen windows, through dill
pickles in wide-mouth pints, garlic cloves
like tiny ivory tusks among fiery tongues
of red-devil chile pods in cider
vinegar—on that same sabbath too hot for hunger
pangs and parables of fishes we did not wish
to multiply, too hot for bread,
for the baking of long, slender, crusted baguettes,

on that day for sipping chilled wine from crystal
side by side with spring water in tin cups—
I know there was a woman
in this same world, a woman not mad,
cruel or violent, who would have gladly died
the full menu of deaths offered here
just for one more mothering day,
one more chance to have taught her child
how even the ravenous scavenger
feasting through flies, nourished by serpent,
moves with such ease
to the painless beauty of food.

Gardens

What kind of flowers are these children,
so familiar to me in polka dot bonnets,
in colorful frocks and shoes black
as taproots clinging to moist soil,
to the life-giving loam. What kind of life,
I wonder, each time I drive through
the Milford Hutterite Colony
to buy vegetables the children sell
as I once sold *Nightcrawlers, 10¢ A Dozen*
back when the doorbell would thrill a boy of five
finding a stranger, grizzled in hip boots,
smiling through the screen.
                                    Sweet Williams?
Are they sweet Williams? Morning glories? Daffodils?
Lilies of the Valley? What are these
ruddy-cheeked Munchkinland lovelies
always giggling in whispered German? *Blue*-eyed
Susans? Zinnias? Petunias? Now I know!
They're my Noni's begonias, her crocuses,
poppies and phlox backdropped by hollyhocks.
                                              Bobbing
through the fertile vegetable beds, the girls
twist and pluck the cukes and zukes,
yank the beets, cut the *cauli-brocci-cauli,*
pull carrots and pinch-off string beans
they carry pouched in turned-up tulip-petal aprons
down the long rows to the tractor-drawn cart,
to the teeniest elfin children
babushkaed and black-capped, riding atop
pumpkins, gourds, hubbard squash, and spuds
all morning, to and fro—from garden
to Quonset hut root cellar.
                                    One fall day
I found them dancing the cabbage to kraut,

fantasia barrels of laughs,
while their mammas shucked corn and sang
with cathedral choir harmony
country-western unrequited love songs
sounding like the psalms—what strange revelation
sometimes comes real on the outer rim
of this thin, predictable life.
                    Face-to-face
with an inkling of their wisdom, I was pointed
toward a bumper crop—Willie, the gardener,
bidding me to *grab them before Jack Frost does,*
to pick to my heart's content. There,
in the enchanted orchard of Better Boy tomatoes,
rosy-cheeked and peeking at me
between the vines, I realized peace
is not a pipe dream or wild wish from the magical
land of Oz or God. I thought again as a child
stretching earthworms from their firm grips
to gardens and flower beds, my flashlight beam
floating ghostly through the dark
backyards of our block, where I hoped for myself,
as I hoped again in the garden of the Hutterites,
that I too might someday resist
the long and lonely pull from home.

For Willie and The Children

I Thought That Hope <u>Was</u> Home

— Emily Dickinson

If hope is home, then poetry's home is made
most hopeful by the root
hair fingers of an oak
woman making herself
even more beautiful as she creates
from her own rib-
branch, from paper and tapered fly line,
thirty pages sewn
into one life. Tree ring, trout stream,
circle and swirl all know this world
was still miracle before words,
but the world before woman was mere
rock, water, wood, dark. A man
blinded by the grace of a gift, I touch
my fingerprint topography
to the map of Montana that fits
the book's cover, taut
as sapling bark. I trace
its ridges and cusps, braille each
crescent lenticel, feel my own breathing
through pores, feminine tempo and rhythm
thrumming from deep
glacial layers rolling
beneath the Rockies' east slope. Drawn
to an old house there, I knock for days
with no answer. I tiptoe in,
inch my way to the horizontal door, lift
it creaking, ease the weight
of one foot through earthen light
onto the top stair. The fine-tipped pen
marking a first letter
into this handmade book, I know
there are no empty homes,
no hopes abandoned, on landscape we love,

on paper we crave and live for. Poems
are the blood of fruit
preserved in rows of dark blue hearts
always pulsing luscious from the cellar.

For Sally Brock

Words Growing Wild in the Woods

A boy thrilled with his first horse,
I climbed aboard my father hunkering in hip boots
below the graveled road berm, Cominski Crick
funneling to a rusty culvert. Hooking
an arm behind one of my knees, he lifted
with a grunt and laugh, his creel harness creaking,
splitshot clattering in our bait boxes.

I dreamed a Robin Hood-Paladin-Sinbad life
from those shoulders. His jugular pulse rumbled
into the riffle of my pulse, my thin wrists
against his Adam's apple—a whiskered knuckle
prickly as cucumbers in our garden
where I picked nightcrawlers, wet and moonlit,
glistening between vines across the black soil.

Eye-level with an array of flies, every crayon
color fastened to the silk band
of his tattered fedora, the hat my mother vowed
a thousand times to burn, I learned to love
the sound of words in the woods—Jock Scott,
Silver Doctor, Mickey Finn, Quill Gordon, Gray
Ghost booming in his voice through the spruce.

At five, my life rhymed with first flights
bursting into birdsong. I loved
the piquant smell of fiddleheads and trilliums,
hickory and maple leaf humus, the petite
bouquets of arbutus we picked for Mom.
I loved the power of my father's stride
thigh-deep against the surge of dark swirls.

Perched offshore on boulder—safe from wanderlust
but not from currents coiling below—

I prayed to the apostles for a ten-pounder
to test the steel of my telescopic pole,
while Dad, working the water upstream and down,
stayed always in earshot—alert and calling to me
after each beaver splash between us.

I still go home to relearn my first love for words
echoing through those woods: *I caught one!*
Dad! I caught one! Dad! Dad!
skipping like thin flat stones down the crick—
and him galloping through popples, splitshot ticking,
to find me leaping for a fingerling, my first
brookie twirling from a willow like a jewel.

5

GRACE

Everything is speaking if we listen. A rock just talks slower. It takes a hundred years for it to say one syllable. We're not around long enough to hear what it has to say.

— Natalie Goldberg

Grace

In the soft low light up high
where love has always thrived and will
forever yearn for the colorful hover—a brush stroke
of words out of the West—we still *want*
free life, we still *want fresh air.*

And as millenniums meander by
like birthdays to the earth, what thrill
a saffron blade of grass, blue sage, scrub oak
still brings us on our daily jaunt
across the land, our daily poem, our prayer.

Love the Color of Trout

Smoldering, after rain all day, the sun
sets fire to saffron yellow logs
the barn hunkers on. Coffee Creek
cuts a swath we hop across,
green to more green,
and whitetail deer, sudden
as stump mushrooms and rust red
with summer hair, browse
brisket-deep—dash of paprika
on this timothy green. We unravel
worms from roots we spade
to the surprise of light. Our fingers
chill pink, and riffles
cater our bait to trout,
to that hearty tug we hunger for
as love: boy and girl in mint
Montana green, willow
Indian stringer of rainbow
swinging in cadence
as we sail the hayfield home.

For Kathy Ogren and Bob Shepherd

For the Stories

Deep blue backdropping the bucolic autumn
embroidery of sumac, maples, spruce
bordering dewy hay meadow sparkling beneath
the sun rising giddier than usual that day
with anticipation, Charlie Parker
steps from his smoky touring car
into the peculiar air of a rural morning,
builds his horn and blows
choruses for a lone cow
because Bird heard animals love
music, too. I picture it this way:
the intimacy of each frosty note
scaling a five-wire fence
between Bird and Holstein—it had to be—
because I can hear Parker telling later
how he blew for *a black cow*
with a little white on it,
maybe for the same reason he played
Hank Williams on the juke,
not for love of rudimentary chords
but *for the stories—just listen*
to the stories, man, he'd tell
his fellow cats razzing him
about his white-blues taste
in tunes. It's pure hearsay
that the puzzled cow—though chewing
her cud in tempo with Bird's
swaying saxophone
shimmering in the low sun, his fingers
slowly crawling over the valves—
was not impressed. I don't buy a word
of it. Rather, I picture a bedraggled farmer
thrilled out of his drudgery
the night Betsy's milk output tripled for life

after an otherwise run-of-the-mill day
when our world moved four bars,
four measures from its normal
orbit, stirring, in turn, the whole
infinite universe toward
the unpredictability of what is
musically possible, humanly perfect.

Light

He cherished the chunk of burled apple
bucked from the trunk
of his grandfather's oldest tree—cured,
stored, packed, and moved it with Audubon art,
alongside Victorian rococo, from home
to new home, through his feisty thirties,
through mid-life crises into his tender fifties
until the wedding of a close friend
brought us to his hearth
one cool Seattle afternoon. We watched him
lay the log onto the grate
cradled with cedar
kindling the color of straw, lay it
gently as a priest placing the swaddled infant
into the manger of the crèche. Lord,
how that apple burl beamed
its radiance behind the bride and groom,
and long after their kiss, still glowed
brighter yet behind him
sitting close to the firelight's shadow play,
the ceiling alive with crows
dancing to the pantomime
of his limber fingers wheeling their excited flight
as he spoke to us of his first love
for rich earth.
                His grandfather taught him,
while planting saplings together
on their knees, to know the loam as sacred
living flesh—to cup it loosely in both hands
embracing it close enough to see,
within its darkness, the starlight,
close enough to hear the high
pitch a single sparkling granule sings
shifting into its new, unique niche

in the universe—until once, so charmed
while savoring the sweet
sweet breath, he barely caught himself reaching the pink
tip of his tongue, like an angleworm,
toward the dirt, his grandfather coaxing him on
with a chuckle. As we laughed, each spark
became a burgundy seed. We relived
with him the bushels of intimate fruit
he knew in his youth, and we too felt
the brisk autumns of first-frost harvests
so real, we flinched at the thought of windfall
thump and bruise.
                    After the last champagne toast,
we left him alone with his embers
living long past midnight
when we dreamt him
sifting through cupped hands
to each sapling in his backyard orchard
the warm ash at dawn, fairy tale
glitter dust, as magical
as photosynthesis itself—this sunlit sprinkle,
this gift of grandfather
friendship passed on
through the family of the rose.

For Fred Lighter

Firewood

A sacrilege against my blue-collar
Catholic manhood, I no longer cut my own
winter supply. I pay 85 a cord
delivered, but I'll be damned
if I'll stand idly by and watch Willy stack it
solo. When he backs-in his flatbed Ford
cornbinder, leaf springs groaning
under the nice jag of dry lodgepole pine,
How she goin' Willy, I ask, after
not having seen him in purt-near a year,
him grinning his big Polish grin,
his porterhouse steak grip swallowing mine,
Good, good, his reply, while apologizing,
in the same breath, for 5-6 blocks
of punky butts he slipped into the load
not knowing he'd be hauling it here. *Just
so she fills a hole in the stack
and makes a little ash,* I laugh back
at him still grinning, his head tipped
almost at rest on his left shoulder, crescent
moon of movie-star-teeth
cradled in a dark-night-sky
weathered face. Without another word,
we go to work
until, on the tailend of the blow we take
two ricks into the load, he opens up,
says *remember how you asked how I was? Well—*
he tosses me one of the punky blocks—
the doc thinks I got prostate cancer,
cancer landing in my hands
with an unexpected heft
yanking me almost to the ground. Burning
barely enough BTUs to keep warm,
we finish the job, drink a cold beer, talk

1957 Impalas and Polish galumpkis
we grew up on—honest 8-by-4-by-4 cords,
chainsaws, sawbones, the Packers, Monday night,
taking on the Vikes at Lambeau, our Green-'n'-Gold
struggling to keep their playoff hopes
alive against long odds. Two fast friends
burning the same wood, watching the same
game on separate television sets
miles apart in our own living rooms, we pull
hard for the unlikely win—believing,
at the same time, there's always next year.

For Willy Puzon

The Antler Tree

For Matt Hansen—In Memoriam

Late at night I braid the helix
from floor to ceiling—skeletal
thicket of deciduous horns,
pillar of prongs, of cambers and angles—
as I drink aged whiskey to the spit
of pitchwood embers in Montana, autumn,
the Rockies cross-stitched
in tamarack yellows, bull elk
bugling their shrill stake
to territory, to harem. The trek
comes back distinct as moon-
silhouetted pine boughs, a rack of antlers
on a ridgetop miles off. It begins with a boy,
with a map he unfolds to trace for me
secret trails to his enchanted land, his trove,
the mother lode of abandoned bone.

One by miraculous one, we found them
almost always rocking on the arc
of main beam, crown tines forked
like hazel dowsing rods peeled white—
widespread fingers gleaming
above green billows of grass
beneath aspen, as if beckoning us
from a hundred paces away. It was easy
to imagine them lightning-
chiseled out of jack pine, a wilderness
wind scattering dry limbs
popped clean from sockets. Some so freshly dropped,
it was easy to believe shamans
laid them in our random paths
seconds ahead of us, to believe grace
a sculpted substance—textured, with heft.

Shoulders galled, collarbones aching, feet blistered
after twelve, uphill, talused miles,
we unlashed each other from antlered packs
and reveled in the weightlessness that tripped
light-headed leaps over treetops, a floating
those trophy bulls must know
shaking both beams free. I hover often
in that dream, looking down at you
finding a matched set of 6-points
seconds apart—their rosettes, flaxen
full moons over August barley,
their scarred tines like scrimshaw
rubbed to an ivory gloss
against sapling pines. You grappled one
gnarled base in each hand
hoisting them with a 12-year-old's wild joy.

Each time I build this tree, I learn,
as a blind child with braille
might learn, the unique interlockings
of a magical language. Tines
clack and rattle into place
like lines we recited along trails
to let bears know the poets
were coming for bone. These antlers, Matt,
having grown branch by branch
more potent. Parts of ourselves
we burnish, then abandon
with hope they'll be gathered
by those who'll keep them whole,
those who'll hear the invisible
clash and clatter through lodgepole—your echoes
making the heart of this hunter pound hard.

And for Ripley, Melissa, and Derek

Measuring

Maybe today she'll know me,
the alfalfa, brome, timothy, and horse
aroma I track in with a limp
to this rest home. Thrown again,
rodeo-old at 30, I visit a pioneer
schoolmarm excused from the world
she risked 90 years. Her skin,
frostbitten leaf,
flinches to the cold touch
of a hot-fudge shake, a favorite
treat I hope will soothe
her scorn for the nightmare fate
she wakes to. She scans this one-room life
in silence, eyes still keen to a horse or boy
who favors one leg. She recites my name,
poised like a pupil answering right,
and then, in slow soliloquy
between sips of chocolate, a child's voice
warns how pain gone dormant wakes
all at once.
                    Through window film
thick as cataracts,
I fix on aspen turning yellow
in the green world of fir
after autumn frost. Children spring up
like a fairy ring—one quick blink—all spunk
from the monkey bars next door. They swing,
teeter, and flip
gymnastic routines to the beat
of laughter and brabble
vanishing into vacant lots.
                        Watching me
watch those children, maybe
she remembers the way memory was

once an easy measure, a finger count,
simple as that certain space
for love —*THIS much!*—we clung to
like a fantasy, a mirage—youth
secure between arms flung wide.

For Sylvia Haight

1998

The first year I ever lost
five dear friends to death, I did not
squeeze off a single shot,
nor set a single hook
or trap. The buck I didn't drop
still works the open slope for feed,
the grouse I didn't bag
are swallowed snowdrift-warm,
and waterfowl I did not decoy-in
catch the final waves of tailwinds
rolling south. That first sad year
I lost five friends to death
the only blood between my fingers
was my own. And the flesh,
fluorescent-lit, I could not get myself
to pick from cellophaned displays
turned grayer than the earth I traipsed
on days when I caught wind
of good friends gone. On those same gray days,
the woman I hold dear fought cancer off
while I fed flocks of songbirds
tons of seed. I began to live
on heavy breads and beers, rice, polenta,
tortilla chips and beans. I planted trees
and had the wild rabbits eating
from my hand. I refused to move
the pickup truck until the purple finches
nesting in its grill
had fledged. Till then, I tossed
the magpies table scraps
to lure them away from chirping
baby birds. In *their* first year,
as I lost five close friends to death
and the money came and went

right down the drain, my lover's hair,
shed in clumps upon her pillow,
became the auburn weft of robins' nests
while mine got thinner by the minute
till it no longer hid the shine. This year,
the last of the millennium, maybe—just *maybe*—
I'll hunt and fish again,
invite ten new friends for dinner
and a lesson in the finer art
of letting go, of holding on and on.

> *For Buck, Blanton,*
> *Richard, Ray, Lila Mae*
>
> *(and Larry Holland)*

Flashback

Please fill my ear with softer sound,
I wish, lifting a thrift store conch shell
one week after the crash and still
cringing to the jagged-edged
noise of chain
collision, to pain in the rotator cuff
of what I will call, till the day I die,
my throwing arm. August gone,
dusk no longer able
to tuck the sultriness of sun
and hold its sweaty warmth up
under Montana's hefty September moon, I am drawn
from the sea I could not hear
to a wooden Pabst Blue Ribbon box
stored in a cobwebbed corner of the garage
so sentimentally empty
without our family car. I stand in its space.
I am amazed by the body,
man-made or otherwise, surviving
on its original four-banger heart
umpteen years, a quarter million miles,
all warranties, rebates, guarantees,
long ago expired.
                    The crumpled Rawlings football
flops from the beer box with no more bounce
than hockey skates and fielder's mitt
onto the concrete slab. I spit
in my palm, wet the needle, work it
clockwise into the stiff valve and witness
leather—unlike glass or metal—
taking back its shape. My grip fits
the laces with a craving
for simplicity fulfilled. I throw the pump-fake,
then perfect spiral. Across the pasture,
a pair of colts watch the pigskin
launching almost vertical,

just a bit more trajectory each time
until I can not quite race under it
to make the fingertip snag, a boy's
playful hands atrophied
to hooves. I think better of the Hail Mary pass
toward my tailback receivers
trotting rocky ground
into the sunset.
                    I must have thought *cortege*—
blinded as my head snapped back
to track the next toss, whiplash
shooting again through the trapezius,
and two geese surprising my eye
where the ball once flew—I must have sensed
at that sad moment the dying
Princess in a Paris tunnel with her mate
already dead, the dark blue
Mercedes demolished
one week to the hour after we walked
away from similar aftermath, body and soul
out of the blurred midst of the twisted.
                                      The ball
disappears into the crown of a Lombardy
poplar bobbling it just
long enough for me to slide
my splayed hand
between leather and earth, knuckles
skinned. Because summer barely hangs on yet
in branches fleshed thick and breaking
the fall, today this is what life takes
and death gives back—the split-
second intimacy inside a car spinning
out of control, hit and hit again and still
spinning as I learn
what thin significant space
a single leaf, love
passing before our eyes, fills.

For One Micro-Chronon of Time

Not the collisions and mirror image story-
caving-in-upon-story
collapsings of all hope,
but rather *this* footage is what
we must run and rerun
to believe we can live on. Notice—this time,
your eyes closed, your heartbeat
stilled—how those there witnessing
the one-by-one acceleration of the towers' top floors
buckling, all threw their arms up
in New York unison. Against the looming black
weight, imagine, feel, how they strained
to lock into place with their power-
lifting lumbar—with their knees,
shoulders, elbows, fingers, toes,
sinew and soul—the tonnage
they knew they could hold aloft
like the song's superhuman coal miner hero,
Big Bad John, hoisting a timber
while trapped men *scrambled*
from their would-be graves. Mere geologic
disaster of earth and rock,
it's true, is a far far cry
from thick concrete, steel girder, plate glass
falling from love and hate
forces locking horns so high above
not even the most faithful incarnate should hope
to hold back the heavy downpour of hearts
stopping cold. But they did. Watch closely
this time-lapse frame-
by-frame replay

pulsing so, so slow, and you, too, will
believe how they held, for the most truthful
infinitesimal moment, the whole
world's molecular make-up
of evil at bay—how they held, and they held.

Bless the Gentle

Try to imagine this sad planet saner
graced only by their kind,
not one thought idle enough
to betray garden and art, to shirk
play and freedom
in favor of greed. Though we can't count
ourselves among them, let us mourn
the concocting of gunpowder, the unearthing
of motorcars, the inventing of what's been dubbed
legal tender.
        Despite those of us
dressed in tweed, plaid, khaki,
denim, poly, camo, try to imagine
the gentle holding fast in their nakedness,
though more defenseless than ever. Their spirit
prospers in the Pueblo
offspring of Anasazi, in children
of the shrinking rain forest, in sequoia
and redwood cambiums, in sphagnum
mosses, rock lichen, rollicking
acrobatics of baleen whales—even
perhaps in the paramecium—and most frail,
yet adamant, of all, in the platypus
and manatee.
        What colossal will
persists in the koala, gripping eucalyptus
canopies high among galahs—in all
songbirds, raptors, the chimpanzee, the panda
rocking on its haunches,
the silverback gorilla. What great loss
we will someday come to feel
bowing to the picturebook wistful
glimpses of those allowed to go
extinct.
        Looking through an upstairs window,

I delight in the whitetail
doe with twin fawns
nibbling timothy, seeming to tiptoe
deliberately into the heartland
of my reflection, into the gentle
drumbeat giving thanks.

For Gennie Nord

One Sweet Evening Just This Year

Sundown rolling up its softest nap
of autumn light over the foothills, grass
bales stacked two tiers above the '69 Ford cab,
our long-toothed shadow slices east,
mudflaps dragging dry gumbo ruts
back home after one beer
at the Buckhorn Bar quenched the best
thirst I've worked-up
all millennium, pool balls
clacking above the solemn
cowmen reminiscing their scripture,
waxing poetic lines to the The Legend
of Boastful Bill—*one sweet morning*
long ago, the hands-down favorite. I'll bet
this whole load, that old bard,
Charles Badger Clark, knew the eternal
bent of those words
the instant he scratched them across the open
range of the blank page.
                              Glacial melt
runneling over mountain rock,
moist air swirls in the cab
stirring up three decades of Montana
essences atomized
into a single mist, this horse-cow-dog-grit-
gunpowder-drought-leather-sage-sweat-
smoke-loss-whiskey-romance-song
fragrance settling upon the porous
inner wrist of dusk
unfolding for only a moment
its sweet, unique blossom.
                              And me, tonight
I'm the lucky one along for the ride,
head still sweaty beneath my hat,

a harlequin glitter of hayseed
sticking to my bare arm stretched straight
out the window for no reason
but to know my own pores rising
beneath hair pressed flat
and flowing like grass in crick-bend shallows,
timothy in the side mirror, stems hanging on
with one arm and waving
wild with the other—to golden meadows
and rolling prairie flecked with cattle,
antelope, jackrabbit, grouse,
all grazing beneath one big gray
kite of bunched starlings'
acrobatic flashings over stubble.
                                        We mosey home,
me and the old truck, in love
with our jag of good Montana grass—
not one speck of simplistic myth
between us and the West that was, sometimes
still is, and thus will be
forever and ever, amen.

For Ralph Beer and Wallace McRae

ACKNOWLEDGMENTS

The author and publisher salute the editors of the literary journals and magazines in which a number of poems from this collection were debuted:

Michelle Stevens-Orton and Allen Jones—**Big Sky Journal**: *The Meaning of Intimacy, Heart's Dressage, Equine Houdini, Bringing Home the Poems, Potatoes, Cowboys & Indians, Sister Sundays, Gardens, Love the Color of Trout.*

Hilda Raz—**Prairie Schooner**: *Playing Favorites, Flight, Living in Snake Country, The Day the War Began, Tsankawi, Light, Flashback.*

Joe Parisi—**Poetry**: *Angelina, My Noni's Name Means Messenger, The Antler Tree, Measuring.*

Kirk Robertson—**Neon**: *The Hand, Shoes.*

Jim Barnes—**The Chariton Review**: *1998.*

Red Shuttleworth & Larry Holland—**Elkhorn Review**: *Bucks in Rut*

Ray Gonzalez—**The Bloomsbury Review**: *Wings.*

Kent Anderson—**Cold Drill**: *Carnivore.*

Our gratitude as well to the editor-publishers of the following books and chapbooks:

Tracks—Emily Strayer, The Kutenai Press, 1989: *Las Ballenas de Bahia Magdalena, Wings, Tracks, How the Beluga Spoons, The Antler Tree.*

Roughstock Sonnets—Payson Lowell, The Lowell Press, 1989: *Measuring.*

The Garnet Moon—Bob Blesse, The Black Rock Press, 1990: *The Garnet Moon, Tsankawi.*

I Am Not a Cowboy—John Dofflemyer, Dry Crik Press, 1995: *The Meaning of Intimacy, The Day the War Began, Shoes, The Hand.*

Blue-Collar Light—Quinton Duval, Red Wing Press, 1998: *Antipasto!, Words Growing Wild in the Woods.*

The poem *Grace* initially appeared on the 2000 National Cowboy Gathering poster, published by the Western Folklife Center.

Cowboy Poetry Matters: From Abilene to the Mainstream, an anthology, edited by Robert McDowell, Story Line Press, 2000, included the poems: *One Sweet Evening Just This Year, Putting the Rodeo Try into Cowboy Poetry, Bizarzyski—Mad Bard and Carpenter Savant of Manchester, Montana—Feeds the Finicky Birds.*

Finally, an extra-high hoist of the Guinness with a hearty *sláinte* to Jim Rooney, who produced the CD, **Words Growing Wild**, and gave voice to: *Shoes, Montana Second Hand, The Hand, Words Growing Wild in the Woods.*

ABOUT THE AUTHOR

Paul Zarzyski migrated west in 1973 from his homeground
in Hurley, Wisconsin to study with poets Richard Hugo
and Madeline DeFrees at the University of Montana, where
he received a Master of Fine Arts degree and, later, taught
creative writing. His published work includes, *The Make-Up
of Ice* (University of Georgia Press, 1984), *All This Way for
the Short Ride* (Museum of New Mexico Press, 1996) which
received the Western Heritage Award for Poetry from the
National Cowboy Hall of Fame, *Blue Collar Light* (Red Wing
Press, 1998) and *Words Growing Wild* (Jim Rooney
Productions, 1998)—a spoken-word CD.

Paul has toured Australia and England, recited at the
National Storytelling Festival, the National Folk Festival,
the Library of Congress and on Garrison Keillor's *A Prairie
Home Companion*. He considers the National Cowboy
Poetry Gathering in Elko, Nevada his second home, and
has been a featured performer there annually since 1987.

Paul lives west of Great Falls, Montana where poetry is
his full-time work.